DAYS THAT SHOOK THE WORLD

THE DREAM OF MARTIN LUTHER KING

28 AUGUST 1963

Liz Gogerly

HODDER
Wayland

an imprint of Hodder Children's Books

DAYS THAT SHOOK THE WORLD

Produced by Monkey Puzzle Media Ltd
Gissing's Farm, Fressingfield
Suffolk IP21 5SH, UK

First published in 2003 by Hodder Wayland
An imprint of Hodder Children's Books
Text copyright © 2003 Hodder Wayland
Volume copyright © 2003 Hodder Wayland

Series Concept: Liz Gogerly
Commissioning Editor: Alex Woolf
Editor: Patience Coster
Picture Researcher: Lynda Lines
Design: Jane Hawkins
Consultant: Michael Rawcliffe

Cover picture: Martin Luther King addressing a rally in Jackson, Mississippi during the
March Against Fear in June 1966 (Corbis/Flip Schulke).

Title page picture: The crowd applauds King's 'I have a dream' speech on
28 August 1963 (Corbis/Flip Schulke).

We are grateful to the following for permission to reproduce photographs:
Associated Press 6, 7, 17 bottom, 20 (Gene Herrick), 23 top (Gene Herrick), 23 bottom, 27 (Horace Cort), 32, 36,
42, 43 top; Corbis 9 (Marion Post Wolcott), 10 top (Bettmann), 10 bottom (Bettman), 15 (Dorothea Lange), 17 top,
18, 19 (Flip Schulke), 21 (Bettmann), 22 (Bettmann), 24 (Bettmann), 28 (Bettmann), 29 (Bettmann), 30 (Bettmann),
31, 33 (Flip Schulke), 34 (Flip Schulke); Hulton Archive 11 (Jack Benton/Archive Photos), 13 (MPI); Popperfoto 25,
37, 39 both, 43 bottom (Reuter); Rex Features 8, 40 right (Dalmas/Sipa); Topham Picturepoint 12 both, 14, 16 (AP),
26 (AP), 38, 40 left (AP), 41 (AP).

Martin Luther King's speeches and writings: All material reprinted by arrangement with the estate of Martin Luther
King Jr., c/o Writers House as agent for the proprietor New York, NY.
Copyright 1963 Dr. Martin Luther King Jr., copyright renewed 1991 Coretta Scott King
Copyright 1967 Dr. Martin Luther King Jr., copyright renewed 1991 Coretta Scott King
Copyright 1968 Dr. Martin Luther King Jr., copyright renewed 1991 Coretta Scott King

Printed and bound in Italy by G. Canale & C.Sp.A, Turin

British Library Cataloguing in Publication Data
Gogerly, Elizabeth
  The dream of Martin Luther King. - (Days that shook
the world)
  1.King, Martin Luther, 1929-1968 2.Civil rights
movements - United States - Juvenile literature 3.United
States - Race relations - Juvenile literature
I.Title
323.1'196'073

ISBN 07502 3565 9

Hodder Children's Books
A division of Hodder Headline Limited
338 Euston Road, London NW1 3BH

CONTENTS

THE TWENTIETH CENTURY HAD ITS fair share of great speakers. The stirring words of President Theodore Roosevelt, Prime Minister Winston Churchill, President John F. Kennedy and the civil rights campaigner, the Reverend Martin Luther King, Jr., echo through to our century. Their speeches made an impact upon historical events and they still have the power to move us today. Perhaps one of the most moving of these great speeches was made on a hot August day in 1963 in Washington DC, USA when King gave his 'I have a dream' speech. The words, delivered in King's deep baritone, were simple and beautiful yet angry and challenging. For the first time, the black people of the United States had a voice, and now that it was finally being heard it had dignity and a morality that struck at the hearts of people throughout the world.

The speech delivered by King that day was the high point of a civil rights event called the 'March on Washington for Jobs and Freedom'. By 1963, the civil rights movement had reached full steam. Earlier that year, black protests in Birmingham, Alabama had forced President John F. Kennedy to propose a new

Dr Martin Luther King, Jr. (centre, with hand raised) links arms with other protesters as he leads the 'March on Washington for Jobs and Freedom'.

The marchers gather in front of the Washington Monument on 28 August 1963.

civil rights bill that would ban segregation in public places and give the federal government the power to enforce new civil rights laws. Millions of people eagerly received news of the bill; but some, especially whites from the US Southern states, were angry. King was determined that the bill would sail through Congress. To raise support, he backed the idea of a peaceful march on Washington DC. In the months leading up to the event, he toured the country and urged his followers to be in Washington DC on 28 August. Everywhere he went, the crowds were caught up on a wave of optimism. Unfortunately, President Kennedy did not share this sentiment. He believed that the march could develop into riots, which would jeopardize the bill in Congress.

On the morning of the march, King looked out of his window at the Willard Hotel. The night before he had stayed up late writing his speech. He had been allocated just eight minutes to speak at the Lincoln Memorial. In that time he wanted to say something that would be remembered by all Americans. He had told his wife, Coretta, that his speech had been influenced by the words of President Abraham Lincoln. But he had been working on another idea too, and he only hoped he had time to say everything he wanted. Below him the crowds were beginning to

flock into Washington DC. The TV news suggested that there were about 25,000 people in attendance – this seemed far short of expected numbers, but it still promised to be the largest civil rights demonstration yet.

King was ready to tell the world about his dream.

A Moment in Time

On 19 November 1863, almost a century before the March on Washington DC, another great orator is speaking to his people. President Abraham Lincoln is giving his 'Gettysburg address'. The occasion is the dedication of the national cemetery at the site of the Battle of Gettysburg in Pennsylvania. Up on the podium, Lincoln begins to speak in his high, reedy voice: 'Four score and seven years ago, our fathers brought forth on this continent a new nation, conceived in Liberty and dedicated to the proposition that all men are created equal.' The crowd applauds loudly. In just three minutes Lincoln manages to express his hopes and dreams for America: '...this nation, under God,' he sums up, 'shall have a new birth of freedom – and that government of the people, by the people, for the people, shall not perish from the earth.'

MICHAEL (HE BECAME MARTIN WHEN he was baptized in 1934) Luther King, Jr. was born on 15 January 1929 in Atlanta, Georgia. It was the era of the Great Depression. Young Michael, however, was born into a comfortable middle-class family. His father, Martin Luther King, Sr., was a preacher at Ebenezer Baptist Church. King, Sr. was a self-confident, committed Christian who had become a leading light in the local black community. At home he was firm but fair, and always provided well for his family. His wife, Alberta was also a devout Christian and brought

love and warmth into the King household. She and her husband provided a secure and happy childhood. Years later, King wrote: 'Life had been wrapped up for me in a Christmas package.'

The Kings soon realized that they had an exceptional son. King, Jr. was sensitive and loving, and was more moved by the poverty he saw on the streets of Atlanta than most children of his age. When he saw black families queuing to buy bread, he was concerned that they might not have enough to eat. He'd ask his parents why, and bombard them with other questions that seemed far beyond his years. At school he was talkative and did well in his classes.

In 1942 King, Jr. started at Booker T. Washington High School where he continued to do well in English and history, and impressed his teachers with his broad vocabulary. In his spare time he was studying how the great orators

King was born at 501 Auburn Avenue, a black area of Atlanta, Georgia. His father's church, Ebenezer Baptist, was on the same street. King's birthplace is now a tourist attraction in Atlanta.

had practised their skills. Although he was small for his age he had a deep, velvety voice that not only helped him to win prizes for oratory but also made him popular with girls.

In 1944, at the young age of fifteen, King, Jr. was accepted by Morehouse College in Atlanta. King, Sr. had studied there too, but King, Jr. wasn't interested in becoming a pastor like his father; he hoped to become a lawyer or a doctor. College challenged King, Jr. and in the course of his studies he found a new appreciation for religion and its prominent part in the life of black Americans – perhaps his future was in religion after all. After his graduation in 1948 he became assistant pastor at Ebenezer Baptist Church. In September 1948 he attended Crozer Theological Seminary (a training college for priests and rabbis) in Chester, Pennsylvania, where he graduated with a degree in religion in June 1951 and won first prize as most outstanding student. Later that year he started postgraduate studies in theology at Boston University in Massachusetts.

Coretta King, née Scott (1927–)

While King studied at Boston University, he met his future wife, Coretta. King was popular with women, but he couldn't find anyone he wanted to settle down with. When he asked a friend if she knew anybody suitable, she suggested Coretta Scott, a music student from Marion, Alabama. 'The four things that I look for in a wife are character, intelligence, personality, and beauty. And you have them all', King told her at the end of their first date. They were married in June 1953. The following year Coretta was awarded her degree in music, but initially gave up thoughts of a career to focus on being King's wife. After her husband's death, she campaigned for a national holiday in honour of his memory. She also set up the Martin Luther King, Jr. Center for Non-violent Social Change, of which she is president.

The Great Depression brought misery to many Americans, but blacks often suffered the most hardship.

In this crowded, segregated classroom in Georgia in the 1940s children of all ages and abilities are taught by one teacher.

Segregation meant that blacks and whites couldn't even share the same water fountain.

FOR COLORED ONLY

IN MANY WAYS KING HAD a privileged childhood and education compared with most black people living in the American South at that time. But from an early age he was forced to confront an unpalatable fact – black people were at the bottom of society's pile. They lived in the worst homes and neighbourhoods, they took the lowest paid jobs (often in the service or manual labour sectors), and segregation laws ensured that blacks living in the South were constantly made to feel inferior. Even the son of a respectable middle-class black family wasn't allowed to eat in the same restaurants, drink at the same water fountains, walk in the same parks, swim in the same pools, or go to the same schools as white people. King couldn't see the latest films either, as 'coloreds only' cinemas usually showed movies a few years after their release.

King's parents tried to protect their children from the segregation and racism that were so deeply embedded in Southern society, but it was impossible to shield them from the hard facts of life. When he was six, King's friendship with two white boys was brought to an abrupt end by the boys' parents, who did not approve of their sons' association with a black child. It was a cruel blow, but King wanted to find out why it had happened. His mother talked to him about racism and about some of the tragedies that had occurred as a result. Her words stayed with King: 'You must never feel that you are less than anybody else. You must always feel that you are somebody.' King never doubted that for a moment, but the hurt he felt made him determined to fight back in his own way: 'When I grow up I'm going to get me some big words.'

As King grew older, the injustices he saw and experienced made him more resentful. On a bus trip at the age of fourteen, he was forced to give his seat to a white passenger. He bubbled with anger as he was made to stand for the 90-mile journey home to Atlanta. On many other occasions he witnessed the terror directed at the black community by the police or the Ku Klux Klan. Innocent people were often beaten up or lynched by mobs of Klansmen dressed in white robes and hoods. Such scenes haunted King, but how was he going to fight such hatred? At college, for the first time in his life, King could discuss the race issue freely. He learned about the Indian leader, Mahatma ('Great Soul') Gandhi, who in 1930 had led

a peaceful march in protest against British rule in India. Inspired by Gandhi's philosophy of non-violence and passive resistance, King believed that he too could confront the problems that faced his people by 'loving' white people: loving rather than hating them was the only way to bring about change.

The Question

" My parents would always tell me that I should not hate the white man, but that it was my duty as a Christian to love him. The question arose in my mind: How could I love a race of people who hated me and who had been responsible for breaking me up with one of my best childhood friends? This was a great question in my mind for a number of years. "

Martin Luther King, Jr. from The Autobiography of Martin Luther King, Jr., *edited by Claybourne Carson.*

The Ku Klux Klan during an initiation ceremony. 'I remember seeing the Klan actually beat a Negro...' wrote King, '... these things did something to my growing personality.'

Men, women and children being taken captive in Africa. The healthiest and strongest were chosen for transportation to the Americas.

WHEN KING'S PARENTS TOLD HIM about segregation, they also told him the long and unsavoury history of slavery. In the ancient world, civilizations such as Babylonia, Egypt, Greece and Rome had acquired slaves through war and kidnapping to help build their empires. The same principle was repeated when European colonists landed in the Americas. In order to tame this wild and promising land, they needed extra hands. The Europeans traded with African chiefs and merchants for African slaves.

In the fifteenth century, the first slaves were brought to America. Most had shared the same fate; they had been captured in their villages, marched in chains to the coast and sold to Europeans. From there, they were crammed into ships with little food and sanitation, and then forced to endure the long journey across the sea to the Caribbean. Many people died before they even reached the destination, often from starvation or disease, but for those who did survive there was more terror to come. In the Caribbean they were 'broken in' and taught how to be slaves, usually by force. Once they had been 'seasoned' they were ready to be taken to America and sold to the highest bidder. For most, this meant a life of servitude with no pay.

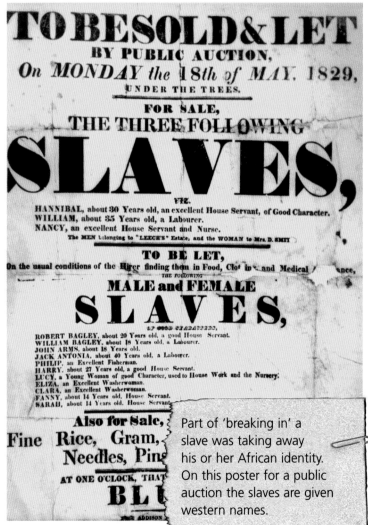

Part of 'breaking in' a slave was taking away his or her African identity. On this poster for a public auction the slaves are given western names.

By the time the slave trade was abolished in the nineteenth century, around 11–12 million African men, women and children had been transported to the American slave colonies. Some 70 per cent of these people were destined initially for the sugar fields of Brazil and the West Indies. By 1820, only two million of the twelve million people who had migrated to the Americas were Europeans; the rest were Africans.

The twentieth-century American writer and black activist W. E. B. DuBois once said, 'We cannot forget that America was built on Africa.' He was remembering the millions of slaves who had been used to make America rich. It was slaves who had worked the fields and raised crops such as coffee, tobacco, sugar and rice, and it was their sweat that had brought the European colonists wealth and prosperity. In the process the slaves had been treated inhumanely and stripped of all liberties. Often they were separated from their families and banned from marrying. They worked long hours under the watchful eye of their overseer, who punished them if they were 'lazy' or rebelled. Usually they slept on mats in huts and were given the worst food to eat.

Laws were later passed which forbade slaves an education, or the right to own property or land. Taken away from their own customs and wrenched from their families, many slaves found solace in Christianity. On some plantations, slaves would hold their own religious meetings, while in towns many joined the Methodist and Baptist churches. Prayers and rousing songs offered some comfort in their bleak lives.

An overseer keeps a close watch over a field of slaves picking cotton in the American South. He would have used a whip on those who stepped out of line or idled.

Cruelties of Slavery

" For more than two centuries our forebears labored in this country without wages; they made cotton king; they built the homes of their masters while suffering gross injustice and shameful humiliation – and yet out of a bottomless vitality they continued to thrive and develop. If the inexpressible cruelties of slavery could not stop us, the opposition we now face will surely fail. We will win our freedom because the sacred heritage of our nation and the eternal will of God are embodied in our echoing demands. "

Excerpt from 'King's Letter From Birmingham Jail', quoted in the Autobiography of Martin Luther King, Jr., *edited by Clayborne Carson.*

IT WAS THE AMERICAN CIVIL WAR, which started in April 1861, that finally brought about the end of slavery throughout the USA. The Civil War began when the Southern states seceded (formally withdrew) from the Union, but it soon turned into a war about the abolition of slavery. On 1 January 1863, President Abraham Lincoln issued the Emancipation Proclamation, which abolished slavery in those states that had seceded; but thousands of slaves remained unfreed in the South. Two years later, following the Union victory, slavery was abolished throughout the USA with the passing of the Thirteenth Amendment to the US Constitution.

The abolition of slavery brought black people freedom from their masters, but it didn't bring them economic security. The South had been devastated by war and there was hardship for everybody, especially for the black population. Poor farmers had to rent their land from white landlords in a system called sharecropping. Although there were white sharecroppers, the majority of them were black. Once again the blacks were at the mercy of the whites and high rents meant they were living in poverty. President Lincoln attempted to bring stability by proposing the redistribution to the blacks of lands that had been confiscated from plantation owners. These plans were thwarted when Lincoln was assassinated in 1865.

President Abraham Lincoln (1809–65)

Abraham Lincoln became American president in 1860, one year before the start of the Civil War. Within months of his taking office, eleven states, mostly in the South, had left the Union. Even though the fight to preserve the Union was his biggest concern, Lincoln was determined to end slavery. He once said: 'If slavery is not wrong, then nothing is wrong.' As president, Lincoln built the Republican Party into a strong national organization. On 1 January 1863 he issued the Emancipation Proclamation that declared forever free those slaves within the Confederacy. By this Proclamation, Lincoln had hoped to initiate slave revolts in the South. However, because the Southern states were rebelling against the Union, the Proclamation was not effective in freeing any slaves. But people such as the black abolition leader, Frederick Douglas, recognized the spirit of the Proclamation and the changes it would bring. Lincoln is remembered as a fair and charitable president and, when he was assassinated on 14 April 1865, many mourned him as a hero. He is still considered by many Americans to have been one of their greatest presidents.

Black men were allowed to fight on the side of the Union from 1862 onwards. They were paid less than white soldiers and often lived in appalling conditions, but at least they were free men.

A black sharecropper and his family arrive home after working all morning on a tobacco farm in North Carolina in 1939.

Between 1865 and 1877, in a period known as Reconstruction, more laws attempted to bring equal rights to black people. In April 1866, a civil rights act was passed that gave slaves citizenship; then, in June 1866, Congress passed the Fourteenth Amendment, which gave blacks the ballot (vote). In March 1870, the Fifteenth Amendment banned racial discrimination in voting. During this period of relative optimism for the black community, some Southern whites became more angry and full of hatred. Poor white sharecroppers became agitated because they were now competing with ex-slaves for jobs. They were also resentful because Reconstruction had been passed by Congress, the government in the North. In 1866, the Ku Klux Klan was formed in Pulaski, Tennessee. Other white extremist groups formed, including the Knights of the White Camellia and the Pale Faces. Now the blacks had poverty and organized violence to contend with.

By 1877 Reconstruction was at an end, and President Rutherford B. Hayes gave some Southern states the right to control their own affairs again. What followed was a series of laws, known as the 'Jim Crow' laws, which chipped away at black people's civil rights by introducing segregation in certain public places. The final blow came in 1896, when a black man called Homer Plessy challenged a Louisiana railroad company in court because they had made him sit in a 'separate but equal' carriage. He charged them with violating his constitutional rights, but he lost the case. With this decision, the US courts had formally sanctioned the segregationist Jim Crow laws. In the years that followed, a stream of segregation laws and stringent black codes were introduced in the South. At all times, blacks had to address whites as Mr, Marse (master) or Miss, while whites called blacks 'boy' or 'girl'. It was as if life had reverted to the way it had been before the Civil War. By the turn of the twentieth century, many poor black people were discriminated against through the introduction of literacy tests, which meant that they could not vote if they were unable to read and write.

By studying the history of slavery, King searched for answers to the problems facing black Americans of his day. He despaired at black people's continued lack of faith in themselves. Years of bending to the will of white masters had, King believed, enslaved their minds, and he searched for a way to free them.

SEGREGATION AND PREJUDICE WERE NOT just a problem in the American South. When life became unbearable for many Southern blacks they migrated to the West and Midwest, or north in search of factory work. Between 1879 and 1890, 58,000 sharecroppers left the South for a brighter future but everywhere they went, segregation and discrimination were a part of their everyday lives. In the North as in the South, blacks were forced to use separate cinemas, lunch counters and water fountains, and live in the worst neighbourhoods. They derived strength from education and religion, founding their own colleges, such as Atlanta University, Fisk University in Nashville, Tennessee (founded in 1866), and Howard University in Washington DC (founded in 1876), and building their own churches. The Methodist Church, the African Methodist Episcopal Zion Church and the Baptist Church (to which King's family belonged) became centres for black communities. Spiritual music and stirring religious oratory, rich in humour, told them they would find peace and justice in the afterlife, which they called the 'promised land'. As the son, the grandson and the great-grandson of Baptist preachers, King too was brought up with a strong religious faith.

However, by the twentieth century, the blacks were fighting back. The black leader William DuBois believed that they could win their cause through the legal system by taking cases of discrimination to court. In 1906 DuBois founded the Niagara Movement, which by 1910 had been renamed the National Association for the Advancement of Colored People (NAACP). In the years to come, the NAACP became

Racial discrimination in New York meant that most blacks lived in a neighbourhood called Harlem. Living conditions were often appalling but in the 1920s Harlem became a centre for black art, literature and music.

the leading organization in the fight for civil rights. In the 1930s King's father was active in the NAACP and had taken part in black demonstrations for equal pay and voting rights in Atlanta. At that time, blacks were still refused the right to vote in national elections if they hadn't paid their poll taxes or passed literacy tests. King Sr.'s involvement in civil rights in Atlanta had earned him respect, even among members of the white community. King was proud of his father and inherited his determination to fight injustice.

In 1953 King was living in Boston with his wife Coretta. He was still studying but was also giving guest sermons at local churches. History had dealt the average black American a poor hand, but King had emerged proud, educated and charismatic and his reputation as a speaker soon spread. At this time King was undecided about his future – perhaps he should teach theology rather than preach – but an event soon occurred that helped make his mind up. In January 1954 he was invited to give a sermon at the Dexter Avenue Baptist Church in Montgomery, Alabama. The church needed a new pastor and hoped that King would be their man. Within months, the eloquent 25-year-old was offered the job. Returning to the South was not an easy decision for King, but he believed he was needed there and he accepted the post on the understanding that he would continue to study on a part-time basis.

King in the mid-1950s, when he was pastor of Dexter Avenue Baptist Church.

Dexter Avenue Baptist Church was a solid brick church not far from the town centre of Montgomery.

A Moment in Time

King and his young wife, Coretta, are back in Montgomery. They are exploring the area of the town where black people live. They look back on their times in Boston and agree that black people have more opportunities there, especially in education. As they look around them now they see how different life will be. They watch a bus drive by and their eyes are drawn to the blacks seated at the back. They realize that they will not only have to sit at the back of Montgomery's buses, but they will also have to stand in line behind the white man for everything else. However, if they turn their backs on the South they may never confront the injustices that exist between blacks and whites, and more than anything King wants to make a difference for his people. Coretta understands her husband's calling. 'If this is what you want,' she tells him, 'I'll make myself happy in Montgomery.'

NAACP members demonstrate against segregation in Chicago during the 1940s. King joined the Montgomery branch of the NAACP in 1954.

BY MAY 1954, KING WAS settling into his new life in Montgomery. In the same month, after years of struggle on the part of the NAACP, the US Supreme Court ruled that segregation was illegal in publicly funded schools. The NAACP had pleaded the case of a black girl called Linda Brown of Topeka, Kansas, who had been barred from an all-white school, and had won their case against the Board of Education. Many whites in the South were outraged and called the day of the ruling 'black Monday'. But for black people throughout the USA it was a turning point – now they hoped to tackle segregation laws everywhere. King was also jubilant; perhaps this was a sign that he'd made the right decision to come back south.

On 1 September 1954, the Kings moved into the parsonage in Dexter Avenue. That autumn, King finished his thesis and started to concentrate on being a full-time pastor. Dexter Avenue was considered by most people in the black community to be a place of worship for the 'big folk' – those black people who had been educated and become successful. King was determined to change that and to attract people from all levels of the black community. He worked hard, waking at 5.30 am each morning, to effect these changes. Very soon the dashing new pastor was attracting larger congregations. Ever mindful of social problems, he insisted that each member became a registered voter and a member of the NAACP. King himself had become an active member of the

Montgomery NAACP and was soon elected one of its leaders. He also joined an interracial group called the Alabama Council on Human Relations. Unlike the NAACP, which fought for civil rights through the courts, the Council believed that integration could only be achieved through education.

In spring 1955, King was awarded his doctorate in theology and became Dr Martin Luther King, Jr. At about the same time, Coretta discovered she was pregnant. King, who had always dreamed of a large family, was delighted. Yolanda Denise was born in November 1955. Although King had hoped for a boy, he was thrilled with the little girl and nicknamed her Yoki. The year 1955 had brought great changes in King's life. As a bright young pastor he had generated a new sense of community and optimism at Dexter Avenue. Other black leaders had noted his active involvement in the NAACP and many were urging him to run for the presidency of the Montgomery group. Becoming a doctor and a father were proud moments too, but at the end of 1955 the most challenging chapter of King's life so far was set to begin.

King with his first child, Yolanda. Such quiet and intimate moments at home with his wife and children would become rarer as King's role in the civil rights movement took over his life.

Social Action

" I took an active part in current social problems. I insisted that every church member become a registered voter and a member of the NAACP and organized within the church a social and political action committee – designed to keep the congregation intelligently informed on the social, political, and economic situations. "

Dr Martin Luther King quoted in The Autobiography of Martin Luther King, Jr.

Throughout 1955, resentment towards segregation on Montgomery's buses was edging towards breaking point. Nearly 70 per cent of all bus passengers were black, yet black customers still suffered the indignity of having to sit at the back and offer their seats up to white people when the 'white' seats were full. Bus drivers hurling insults such as 'black ape' or 'black cow' further inflamed the situation. In March, a black schoolgirl had been handcuffed and jailed for refusing to give up her seat. And, despite promises made by the bus companies to the NAACP, conditions did not improve.

On the morning of 2 December 1955, King received a phone call from E. D. Nixon, another senior member of the Montgomery NAACP. The news was startling – Rosa Parks, a 42-year-old seamstress and secretary of the NAACP, had been arrested for refusing to give up her seat on the bus to a white man. 'I was just plain tired,' she later claimed, 'and my feet hurt.' Nixon had rung King for advice. Was this the moment they had been waiting for, he asked King; could it be time to take action and boycott the buses? King called another Montgomery minister, Ralph Abernathy, and a meeting of local ministers and civic leaders was arranged at Dexter Avenue. At that meeting, a boycott was planned for Monday, 5 December. King had doubts about the use of such tactics, but reasoned that it was the only way to tackle an evil system.

Rosa Parks being fingerprinted following her arrest for refusing to give up her seat on the Montgomery bus. King described her as a woman with 'dignity and self-respect'.

Ralph Abernathy (1926–1990)

Ralph Abernathy was born in Linden, Alabama. He first met Martin Luther King Jr. while serving as a Baptist minister in Montgomery. They worked together during the Montgomery Bus Boycott in 1955, and were close friends for the rest of King's life. He accompanied King on all his major campaigns. Abernathy later served as an officer of the Southern Christian Leadership Conference (SCLC), an organization that extended local protests through the network of black churches in the South.

King had complete faith in his best friend. 'He [King] trusted Ralph like he trusted Jesus,' another SCLC member once said. 'Ralph gave him confidence, security, a strong soul to lean on.' King also recognized the large part that Abernathy played in the civil rights movement. He once said: 'I couldn't do my work if you [Abernathy] were not here with me....' When King was assassinated in Memphis in 1968, Abernathy was at his side. He later became president of the SCLC.

A Montgomery bus travels with no passengers during the boycott. King called the protest a miracle: 'The once dormant... Negro community was now fully awake.'

Working Together

" As we stand and sit here this evening and as we prepare ourselves for what lies ahead, let us go out with a grim and bold determination that we are going to stick together. We are going to work together. Right here in Montgomery, when the history books are written in the future, somebody will have to say, 'There lived a race of people, a black people... a people who had the moral courage to stand up for their rights. And thereby they injected a new meaning into the veins of history and civilization.' **"**

From King's first speech as president of the MIA, 5 December 1955, quoted in The Autobiography of Martin Luther King, Jr., *edited by Clayborne Carson.*

On Monday morning, Coretta called her husband to their front room. The first bus had just sailed past their window, and it was empty! Together they watched the next few buses go by. Except for a handful of white passengers, there was no one on the buses. Later that morning, as King drove towards City Hall where the trial of Rosa Parks was taking place, he was thrilled to discover that the boycott had been supported throughout the city. At her trial, Parks was fined $14, but Nixon filed an appeal. King, Nixon and Abernathy rejoiced when they heard that the case would go to the federal court. Now they saw there was an opportunity for the segregation law to be put to the test.

That afternoon, the boycott leaders met again and formed the Montgomery Improvement Association (MIA). King was appointed president of the MIA and gave his first political speech at a meeting held that night at Holt Street Baptist Church. King was nervous about delivering the speech, which he'd prepared in less than twenty minutes. He needn't have worried, because he was a natural orator and the crowd applauded their new leader. The MIA proposed that the boycott would continue until the bus drivers of Montgomery showed courtesy to their passengers, and that all passengers were seated on a first come, first served basis. It also demanded that black drivers would be employed for predominantly black routes.

Spurred on by the Montgomery Bus Boycott there were similar boycotts throughout the South. In Tallahassee, Florida the people organized car pools and lifts just as they had done in Montgomery.

A Moment in Time

It's a cold day in Montgomery, but the buses are still empty. Seeing an elderly black woman dragging her feet down the road, a pool driver slows down his car and calls out to her.

'Jump in, Grandmother. You don't need to walk.'

'I'm not walking for myself,' says the proud old woman, 'I'm walking for my children and my grandchildren.'

The driver smiles to himself as he moves off. He watches the woman in his rear-view mirror as she carries on walking. It's a funny world, he thinks to himself, when walking becomes the best way of protesting for your rights!

THE MONTGOMERY BUS BOYCOTT LASTED for almost a year as the MIA held out for its demands. Many people walked to work, sometimes as far as twelve miles. Others rode mules or took rides in horse-drawn vehicles. For a short while, black taxi-drivers charged the same fare as the buses. When the local authority banned this practice, the MIA organized a car pool. Private car owners, including white employers, arranged lifts for black workers. At the height of the protest, 50,000 people were finding alternative means of travelling.

Many white people were amazed by the strength of the protest; there had never been anything like it in the South before. They believed the first signs of bad weather would put an end to it, but when the protest carried on throughout the winter days they were amazed. By Christmas, the local business community was losing money because black people were staying away from the shops, not wanting to make the trip without bus transport. There was panic among white business owners and threats were being made against the protestors. On some occasions the police bullied the boycotters, or arrested them for loitering. In the past, fear had been an effective weapon against black people, but now they were showing incredible courage. At twice weekly meetings at Dexter Avenue, King attempted to keep the protestors focused and united. He inspired them by telling them about Gandhi. They too could bring about change, but non-violence was the only way forward.

King leaving court with his wife Coretta at his side on 22 March 1956. Although King had been found guilty of leading the Montgomery Bus Boycott people were celebrating because they were proud of his crime.

As the media followed the progress of the boycott, King stood out as an eloquent and effective leader. But his success was tempered by the stream of anonymous death threats against him. He also suffered police intimidation and, on 26 January 1956, was arrested for driving 5 mph over the speed limit. Unfazed by the attempts to scare him, King stood firm. A few days later, on 30 January 1956, a bomb was thrown on to his front porch. No one was hurt, but an angry crowd of armed blacks gathered outside his home – they wanted revenge. King managed to calm the mob, telling them to remain peaceful. For his own safety, King's parents pleaded with him to leave Montgomery, but by now he had made an important decision. He had committed himself totally to the civil rights movement – even if that decision meant being arrested or killed.

The battle to desegregate the buses of Montgomery was long and hard. During the course of the next year, King was arrested, tried and fined for his efforts. However, by November 1956 the US Supreme Court had ruled that bus segregation in Alabama was unconstitutional. That same month, in a last desperate attempt to intimidate the protestors, the Ku Klux Klan drove through the black neighbourhoods of Montgomery. Rather than retreating behind closed doors, the defiant black community lined the streets

and waved at them. On 21 December 1956, Dr Martin Luther King, Rosa Parks and Ralph Abernathy took the first integrated bus ride through Montgomery. By Christmas that year, black people throughout the South had been inspired to act, and bus boycotts were organized in Birmingham, Tallahassee, Florida and Mobile. At last, the civil rights movement was making a stand!

King sits next to Reverend Glenn Smiley and behind Ralph Abernathy on the first integrated bus ride in Montgomery in December 1956.

DURING THE TWELVE YEARS THAT King fought for civil rights he was arrested more than 120 times, but it was the violence against his people that angered him the most. In January 1957, four churches and two black parsonages in Montgomery were bombed. King was shaken; he simply could not believe that people would bomb churches. Yet still he appealed for non-violence, because he knew that retaliation would only result in more death and injury.

King felt guilty about the attacks, in some way he believed he was to blame, and he struggled to reconcile his Christian beliefs with the aims of the civil rights movement. Following the January bombings, morale in the organization was low, but in an emotional speech delivered at a mass meeting, King tried to bring his people hope. After leading the prayers he told them: 'I hope no one will have to die as a result of our struggle for freedom in Montgomery. Certainly I don't want to die. But if anyone has to die, let it be me.'

In February 1957 King became president of the newly created SCLC (see page 20). At a meeting of the SCLC that month King made his first appeal to US President Eisenhower for a White House conference on civil rights. Now was the time for action – not only had blacks found new self-respect but the consciences of millions of white people had been stirred. But Eisenhower hadn't given the black issue much consideration and, when he didn't respond, King began to talk of a SCLC Prayer Pilgrimage to Washington DC. King was now a national figure – his photograph appeared on the front cover of the February 1957 *Time* magazine. It was obvious that neither he nor the civil rights movement could be ignored.

In the summer of 1957, King led 20,000 marchers on a prayer pilgrimage to Washington DC. In many ways the event foreshadowed the march on Washington that would take place six years later. It involved prominent black figures as speakers, such as the singers Sammy Davis Jr and Harry Belafonte. In his first national

Policemen inspect the damage at Bell Street Baptist Church in Montgomery on 10 January 1957. Later that day King and Abernathy also toured the badly bombed churches.

speech King demanded: 'Give us the ballot and we will no longer have to worry the federal government about our basic rights.'

In September 1957, a civil rights act was hastily pushed through Congress by Senator Lyndon B. Johnson. This act set up the Civil Rights Commission to investigate charges that citizens were being denied the right to vote. But it did little to improve the everyday lives of millions of black Americans, and King was saddened when violence erupted in Little Rock, Arkansas, as black students attempted to enrol at the Central High School. Eventually, in an atmosphere of tension, the pupils were escorted through the school gates under the protection of one thousand federal troops. The fight went on, and in October King proposed a 'Crusade for Citizenship'. This time he aimed to get two million black people to register for the vote before the next presidential election in 1960.

Voting Rights

"It was my firm conviction that if the Negro achieved the ballot throughout the South, many of the problems which we faced would be solved. Once we gained the ballot, we would see a new day in the South. I had come to see that one of the most decisive steps that the Negro could take was a short walk to the voting booth."

King writing about the Crusade for Citizenship, quoted in The Autobiography of Martin Luther King, Jr., *edited by Clayborne Carson.*

Black students are escorted to school by federal troops in Little Rock, Arkansas on 1 October 1957.

Lunch-counter protestors faced police intervention and humiliation from whites. These students are undeterred even when racists pour sugar over their heads.

Struggle For Liberation

" A generation of young people has come out of decades of shadows to face naked state power; it has lost its fears, and experienced the majestic dignity of a direct struggle for its own liberation. These young people have connected up with their own history – the slave revolts, the incomplete revolution of the Civil War, the brotherhood of colonial colored men in Africa and Asia. They are an integral part of the history which is reshaping the world, replacing a dying order with a modern democracy. "

King's defence of the sit-ins, made in the magazine Newsweek, *20 February 1960.*

IN JANUARY 1960, KING GAVE his last service at Dexter Avenue before moving to Atlanta. The decision had not been easy – he hated the idea of leaving Montgomery – but the headquarters of SCLC were based in Atlanta and he needed to concentrate on the forthcoming Crusade for Citizenship. Once again he became co-pastor at the Ebenezer Baptist Church. The hard work of the previous year and a near-fatal attempt on his life by a woman in February 1959 had exhausted him, but there was still more for him to do in preparation for the November 1960 presidential election. State laws ruled that, to register as voters, people had to pass literacy tests and prove they had paid poll taxes. This system, which was biased against uneducated and impoverished blacks meant that, of the five million blacks of voting age who were eligible to vote, only 1.3 million were registered. The desegregation of schools was not progressing either. At the start of 1960, only 4 per cent of black students in the South had gained admission to white schools. There had been no major victories in the civil rights movement since Montgomery, and people were getting restless.

However, in early 1960 something spectacular happened. It began in February when a group of black college students studying in Greensboro, North Carolina, organized a sit-in at the segregated lunch counter of a Woolworth's store.

King is welcomed home following his release from jail on 27 October 1960. At his side are his wife Coretta and his young children, Yolanda and Martin Luther III.

The group had acted spontaneously and refused to move until they were served. Despite intervention from the police, the students remained peaceful but turned up the next day to protest again. Throughout the South, black and white students followed their example and staged sit-ins and boycotts at cafés and stores.

King was proud of the students and urged them to form an organization to co-ordinate the protests. In the years that followed, the Student Non-violent Co-ordinating Committee (SNCC) organized sit-ins involving 50,000 students. Its aim was to fill up the jails and, between 1960 and 1963, 24,000 protestors were arrested. Another black group, the Congress of Racial Equality (CORE) staged similar protests at lunch counters, parks, beaches and theatres. Although CORE and the SNCC were not part of the SCLC, both groups followed King's example of peaceful protest. Many members carried signs with the words: 'Remember the teachings of Jesus, Gandhi and Martin Luther King.'

In June 1960, King met with John F. Kennedy, the slick, young Democratic presidential candidate. Kennedy was white and a Catholic. Although King was sceptical about

him, he thought he was honest, and believed he might help the civil rights movement if he was elected. At a student sit-in in Atlanta that October, King was arrested and sentenced to four months' hard labour. Kennedy saw an opportunity to gain black support in the upcoming election and stepped in to help get King released. King praised Kennedy for his part in this, and when Kennedy was elected president on 9 November 1960, King hoped he had found a powerful ally. But he was to be disappointed when Kennedy shied away from introducing civil rights legislation to Congress.

John F. Kennedy (1917–63)
Robert F. Kennedy (1925–68)

Born in Brookline, Massachusetts, the Kennedy brothers were the sons of the rich and influential US businessman and diplomat, Joseph Kennedy. When John F. Kennedy became president of the United States in 1960 he appointed his younger brother, Robert, as attorney general. As educated whites from a privileged background, neither man had much idea of what it was like to be poor, let alone black. However, Robert Kennedy in particular had a sensitivity towards the 'underdog' which eventually led to his championing the civil rights cause. His brother, John, was more cautious, and proposed the civil rights bill only when he believed it had a chance of success in Congress.

When President John F. Kennedy was assassinated in 1963, some people suggested that it was the work of right-wing extremists in protest against the civil rights bill. This suggestion was just one of many conspiracy theories that surround his murder to this day. Robert F. Kennedy was also assassinated in 1968 during his own campaign to become US president.

A Moment in Time

The advertisement on TV for the Funtown amusement park makes it look so exciting. Yoki runs down the stairs to tell her father all about it.

'They say everybody is invited!' Her eyes light up. 'Please can we go, Daddy?'

Martin Luther King looks down at his six-year-old daughter. Many years ago his own parents had had the difficult job of trying to explain to him about segregation. Now, he must tell his own child about an unfair system which means that black children cannot enjoy Funtown because only white people are allowed to visit. For the first time in a long while, he is lost for words.

'I'm so sorry we can't go, Yoki,' he says gently as her bright eyes fill with tears. 'I know it's difficult for you to understand why we can't go, but one day I hope that we can change the rules. But until that time, Yoki, please don't get bitter. Not all white people are to blame. And, never forget, you have to be proud of who you are.'

ANOTHER EMERGING BLACK VOICE IN the 1950s and 1960s was that of Malcolm X, the leader of the Black Muslim group. From his base in Detroit, Malcolm X spoke out against white supremacy and criticized King and other civil rights leaders for their non-violent protests. On occasions he called King a 'chump', and derided his pacifism: 'No man can speak for Negroes who tells Negroes love your enemy,' he argued. 'There's no Negro in his right mind today who's going to tell Negroes to turn the other cheek.' Although Malcolm X generated much support in the North, King's message of peaceful protest continued to influence the civil rights movement. Also, in early 1961, another kind of peaceful protest was about to begin.

The Freedom Rides were organized by the SCLC, SNCC and CORE in an attempt to desegregate the bus and railway stations in the South. On 14 May 1961, two buses carrying four black and four white freedom riders departed from Washington DC on route for New Orleans. The plan was to stop off at stations along the way and desegregate the toilets and lunch counters simply by using them. The riders had already succeeded in using facilities in Virginia and North Carolina, but later that day the second bus encountered a violent mob of Ku Klux Klan members. Armed with guns, baseball bats and knives, the Klan smashed the windows of

Freedom riders escape a burning bus at Anniston, Alabama on 14 May 1961.

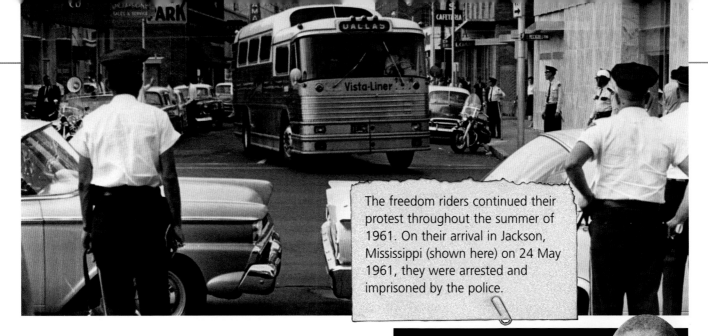

The freedom riders continued their protest throughout the summer of 1961. On their arrival in Jackson, Mississippi (shown here) on 24 May 1961, they were arrested and imprisoned by the police.

the bus before setting fire to it and attacking those who escaped. The first bus was also ambushed in Birmingham and the riders were beaten with lead piping and chains.

The media captured the full horror of events and all around the country people reeled with shock. The Attorney General, Robert Kennedy, had watched the harrowing scenes on television and worked quickly to get the riders some police protection. Unfortunately, when a third, replacement bus (sent out by Robert Kennedy) arrived in Montgomery on 20 May, there were no police to protect its occupants from the one thousand whites armed with guns and knives. Once again, TV cameras rolled as the freedom riders were subjected to vicious attacks.

In response to such violence, Malcolm X urged blacks to 'take whatever steps are necessary to defend themselves'. Meanwhile King hurried to Montgomery to give his support for the freedom riders. On 21 May, on the orders of Robert Kennedy, federal troops were hastily brought in to break up a crowd of angry whites that had gathered outside the First Baptist Church where King was scheduled to speak to the freedom riders. It was a frightening brush with danger, but King stood tall once more (he later became the chairman of the Freedom Riders Co-ordinating Committee). That summer, more than 400 freedom riders were arrested and three were murdered. The situation seemed to be spiralling out of control and Robert Kennedy urged King to stop the riders. King was angry about Kennedy's inability to understand the situation, and refused to back down. It was a tactic that paid off because, in November, Kennedy requested that new regulations should end segregation on transport and in the stations.

Malcolm X (originally Malcolm Little (1925–65)

Malcolm X was born in Omaha, Nebraska. In his early years he was caught up in petty crime, violence and drugs, but in jail he met Elijah Muhammad, the leader of the Black Muslim group. Under Muhammad's influence, Malcolm X changed his name and gave up his Baptist religion for Islam. After his release from jail in 1952, Malcolm X became a leading spokesman for the Black Muslim organization. He believed in Black Power, and regularly spoke out against King and non-violence: 'The white man pays Reverend Martin Luther King… so that Reverend Martin Luther King can continue to teach the Negroes to be defenseless… be defenseless in the face of one of the most cruel beasts that has ever taken a people into captivity'. In 1963, after a series of disagreements with Muhammad, Malcolm X was suspended from the Black Muslims. He founded the Organization for Afro-American Unity, which was based on an alliance between blacks and other non-white groups. After joining a pilgrimage to Mecca in the last year of his life he came to believe that there could be a brotherhood between blacks and whites. But in 1965, following threats against his life by rival Black Muslims, he was assassinated in Harlem, a neighbourhood of Manhattan. Three Black Muslim members were convicted of his murder.

A peaceful march against segregation turns into a nightmare as the police turn powerful fire hoses on the demonstrators in Birmingham, Alabama on 3 May 1963.

I N THE EARLY 1960s DIVISIONS began to appear in the civil rights movement. These divisions were essentially between King and Malcolm X. There were also conflicts between King and younger militants from SCLC and SNCC. Radicals like Malcolm X believed that only revolution could bring social reform, but King still supported peaceful protest. When it came to a civil rights bill, however, King's efforts to get it made law met with a brick wall.

In 1962 King found himself in jail again, for leading a march in Albany, Georgia. Albany was one of King's most crushing defeats. Despite the boycotts and jailing of thousands of blacks, the government had not changed its segregation laws. Non-violence was not working, and King was disappointed, but by learning from the errors made in Albany, civil rights activists were able to plan a more ambitious campaign in Birmingham, Alabama. 'It [Birmingham] is the most thoroughly segregated city in America,' King told the SCLC, 'All the evils and injustices the Negro can be subjected to are right there in Birmingham'. By April 1963 the SCLC had drawn up its Birmingham Manifesto, which included demands for desegregation and more jobs for blacks. When demonstrations began later that month, the local police turned fire hoses on the protestors and made hundreds of arrests. At a peaceful march on 12 April 1963, King was also arrested. This time he was placed in solitary confinement, where he wrote his famous 'Letter from a Birmingham Jail' (see page 13).

The crusades in Albany and Birmingham had kept King in the headlines throughout 1962 and 1963. Some people believed King to be a hero of the civil rights movement, while others believed he was a communist and trouble-maker. Whatever people believed, public opinion was about to be swayed by shocking images that would pour out of Birmingham. Upon his release from jail, King organized more marches but this time he decided to let the children make a stand. On 2 May 1963, 1,000 children marched into the city. By the end of the day, 900 children had been arrested and were practically filling the local jails. 'This is a fulfilment of a dream,' King commented, 'for I have always felt that if we could fill the jails... it would be a magnificent expression of the determination of the Negro.'

The next day the dream turned into a nightmare when police used fire hoses, police dogs and cattle prods on 2,500 children. Images of children screaming as powerful jets of water pounded them to the floor flashed around the world. King had always predicted that television would awaken America's conscience, and in the following weeks the world watched as the country struggled to understand the racism embedded in its society. A few days later more drama followed. The motel in which King had stayed was bombed, along with his brother's church. Peaceful protests degenerated into violent riots as the black community fought back.

In panic, King called President Kennedy and urged him to send in federal troops. This time Kennedy responded, sending in the army. In June the US president made his famous civil rights speech (see panel on this page) and proposed a strong new civil rights bill. That same evening King told the press about plans for a March on Washington DC. The idea for the 1963 March on Washington was inspired by a similar march organized by a black activist called Philip Randolph in 1941. That March on Washington DC had been to campaign for jobs for black people in the wartime armaments industry. The March was cancelled when President Roosevelt gave in to the demands. Ever since, Randolph had dreamed that such a march would eventually take place.

President John F. Kennedy addresses the nation about the civil rights crisis in Birmingham, Alabama on 11 June 1963.

Kennedy on Freedom

"It is as old as the Scriptures and as dear as the American Constitution. The heart of the question is whether all Americans are to be afforded equal rights and equal opportunities; whether we are going to treat our fellow Americans as we want to be treated.... Who among us would be content to have the color of his skin changed and stand in his place? Who among us would then be content with the counsels of patience and delay?... I shall ask Congress... to make a commitment it has not fully made in this century to the proposition that race has no place in American life or law. "

From John F. Kennedy's speech on civil rights, televised on the evening of 11 June 1963.

28 August 1963: The March on Washington

On 28 August 1963, King waves at the massive crowd before him. It was images like these that moved people all around the world.

Presidential Mall, and in the surrounding streets there were thousands more edging their way towards the Lincoln Memorial. In that crowd were poor blacks who had travelled up from the South. Members of one group from Mississippi were marching in their well-pressed overalls. King was moved by their pride and determination to demonstrate. There were also white people in the throng: teachers, students, clergymen and ordinary workers were showing that they cared for the plight of black people.

About 12.00 pm In the White House, President Kennedy and his brother Robert watched as events unfolded on television. Kennedy had given the march his approval, but he was anxious that it might get out of control. Extra police had been pulled in, alcohol sales had been banned for one day, and the army had been placed on alert. But the television images gave Kennedy heart. There was a joyousness and dignity about the event. Many people sang freedom songs like 'We Shall Overcome', while others relaxed and ate picnics on the grass.

About 12.30 pm The atmosphere heightened as more people flooded into the Mall. Film stars like Charlton Heston, Sidney Poitier, Burt Lancaster, Marlon Brando and Harry Belafonte, and famous singers such as Sammy Davis, Jr. and Judy Garland added glamour to the occasion. Later, there would be entertainment too, when singers like Mahalia Jackson, Joan Baez and Bob Dylan would entertain the crowd.

About 1.00 pm Accompanied by his wife and other members of the SCLC, King arrived at the Mall behind the White House. There were now at least 250,000 marchers, 60,000 of whom were white. They gathered on the grass behind the White House and in the park near the Washington Monument. There were people from all races, old, young, rich and poor. Whoever they were, King was pleased to see them. He knew that many had

About 11.00 am King paced nervously around his suite at the Willard Hotel, awaiting word from the march organizers. Without a huge turnout, he feared that the event would be a flop. By all accounts the television report had been wrong though. More than 90,000 people had already gathered on the lawns around the

taken time off work to be there. Many had taken organized 'freedom buses' or 'freedom trains', but others had used the little money they had to pay their fare to Washington DC. He beamed with pride and delight as he made his way slowly towards the Lincoln Memorial and the stage in front of it.

(1.30 pm) Philip Randolph introduced the programme. 'Fellow Americans, we are gathered here in the largest demonstration in the history of this nation,' he told the crowd. A group of US senators and representatives joined him on the stage, together with King and other members of civil rights groups. There was a loud cheer and people began chanting: 'Pass the bill! Pass the bill!' As the first notes of 'The Star-Spangled Banner' filled the air, King surveyed the scene before him. He was overwhelmed with emotion.

People of many different backgrounds, races and political persuasions gathered to hear the speakers. At the end of the reflecting pool behind them stands the Washington Monument.

What Was Demanded in the March on Washington DC

- The passage of 'meaningful' civil rights legislation – no filibustering (delaying tactics).

- The immediate elimination of all racial segregation in publically funded schools throughout the nation.

- Protection for civil rights demonstrations everywhere against police 'brutality'.

- A big programme of public works to provide jobs for all the nations's unemployed.

- A federal law prohibiting racial discrimination in hiring workmen – either public or private.

- $2-an-hour minimum wage, across the board, nationwide.

- Self-government for the district of Columbia, where Negroes make up 57 per cent of the population.

33

About 1.35–3.00pm Other speakers that day included Roy Wilkins of the NAACP. He told the crowd to keep protesting but he urged them to do so peacefully: 'You've got religion here today. Don't backslide tomorrow.' John Lewis of the SNCC gave one of the most biting speeches: 'By the force of our demands, our determination and our numbers,' he told the crowd, 'we shall splinter the segregated South into a thousand pieces, and put them back together in the image of God and Democracy.'

About 3.00 pm In the melting heat of the day, the crowd became restless. They wanted to hear 'the Doctor' speak. When King finally moved towards the microphone a great roar of applause went up from the swarm of people below. 'Five score years ago a great

There was a brief lull after King's speech before the crowd burst into spontaneous applause and celebration.

American, in whose symbolic shadow we stand today, signed the Emancipation Proclamation,' he began in his rich, velvety baritone. 'This momentous decree came as a great beacon light of hope to millions of Negro slaves who had been seared in the flames of withering injustice.... But one hundred years later, the Negro still is not free.' There were many whoops and cheers from the audience as King told them of his hopes, and all the despair he'd harboured for years. 'America has given the Negro a bad check [cheque]; a check which has come back marked "insufficient funds",' he told them. 'Now is the time to make real the promises of Democracy,' he demanded, 'Now is the time to lift our nation from the quicksands of racial injustice to the solid rock of brotherhood... '

King spoke for more than nineteen minutes, but there was one part of his speech, a refrain that had not been rehearsed or written down, that moved the crowd like nothing else that day. In the spirit of the moment, King reached into his soul and told the world: 'I have a dream...' As he told them of his dream for a brighter future for his children, and as he prayed for freedom, King's voice reached new heights. He punched the air, and towards the end of the speech reached on tiptoe as if up to heaven.

In the moments afterwards there was utter silence as King's great words sank in.

The dream of Martin Luther King was for racial harmony and equality, and he urged his followers to pursue this dream peacefully and with dignity. His hopes were so reasonable that it is easy to understand why so many people embraced them.

King has been praised as a hero and a peacemaker. The day he gave his famous speech has become legendary, and his memory has been romanticized. King's words are remembered for their optimism and beauty, but behind the rich language there spoke an angry man. Although he told the world about his dream, he was, in fact, showing them a nightmare.

The Essence of the Dream

" There are those who are asking the devotees of civil rights, 'When will you be satisfied?' We can never be satisfied as long as the Negro is the victim of the unspeakable horrors of police brutality. We can never be satisfied as long as our bodies, heavy with the fatigue of travel, cannot gain lodging in the motels of the highways and the hotels of the cities. We cannot be satisfied as long as the Negro's basic mobility is from a smaller ghetto to a larger one. We can never be satisfied as long as a Negro in Mississippi cannot vote and a Negro in New York believes he has nothing for which to vote. No, no, we are not satisfied, and we will not be satisfied until justice rolls down like waters and righteousness like a mighty stream.

"I have a dream that one day even the state of Mississippi, the desert state sweltering with the heat of injustice and oppression, will be transformed into an oasis of freedom and justice.

"I have a dream that my four little children will one day live in a nation where they will not be judged by the color of their skin but by the content of their character.

"I have a dream today.

"I have a dream that one day the state of Alabama… will be transformed into a situation where little black boys and black girls will be able to join hands with little white boys and white girls and walk as sisters and brothers.

"When we let freedom ring, when we let it ring from every village and every hamlet, from every state and every city, we will be able to speed up that day when all of God's children, black men and white men, Jews and Gentiles, Protestants and Catholics, will be able to join hands and sing in the words of the old Negro spiritual, 'Free at last! free at last! Thank God almighty, we are free at last!' "

Excerpts from King's speech at the Lincoln Memorial.

King's speech brought the programme to a fitting end. Within half an hour of his closing words, only a couple of thousand marchers were left in the area around the Lincoln Memorial. Most people were on their way home, rejoicing his words and filled with new hope. With tears in his eyes, Philip Randolph described it as the most beautiful day of his life. Meanwhile King and the other march leaders left to meet President Kennedy at the White House.

When Kennedy had first heard of the March he'd said: 'Yes, I'm for the bill, but I am damned if I will vote for it at the point of a gun.' However, when King entered the White House, Kennedy went straight up to him and shook his hand. 'I have a dream,' he told King and reassured him that the civil rights bill had his full support. Later, when Kennedy heard that no one had eaten lunch, he arranged for sandwiches and drinks to be served and everyone sat round happily eating and reflecting on a spectacular day.

The media coverage was possibly more extensive than that of any other US political demonstration. The international press covered the day from every angle,

and TV cameras filmed what would become one of the first events to be transmitted live throughout the world. The speech was undoubtedly the highlight of the day, and has become one of those defining moments in history – people remember where they were and what they were doing when it occurred. But the day was a triumph in other ways too. For the first time, thousands of blacks and whites had marched together under one banner, and they had done so without violence. There had been no major disturbances, and just a handful of arrests. The army that had stood by at Kennedy's request had never once been needed. The day helped to undo the damage caused by the appalling images of children being hose-piped just months earlier in Birmingham.

The celebrations lasted through the night – on the streets, and back at the Willard Hotel to which King had returned to share his elation with Coretta and close friends. The rejoicing carried on the next morning when the success of the march on Washington DC was acclaimed on the front pages of practically every local and international paper. But not everyone saw it so positively. Malcolm X called it

President Kennedy welcomed King and the March organizers into the White House following the speech. Pictured from third left to right are: Whitney Young, Jr. (Urban League); Martin Luther King, Jr. (SCLC); John Lewis (SNCC); Rabbi Joachim Prinz (American Jewish Congress); Dr. Eugene Carson Blake (National Council of Churches); A. Philip Randolph; President Kennedy; Walter Reuther (United Auto Workers). Behind: Vice President Johnson and Roy Wilkins (NAACP).

Different Views

" How was a one-day 'integrated' picnic going to counter-influence these representatives of prejudice rooted deep in the psyche of the American white man for four hundred years? "

Malcolm X's comment on the March on Washington DC, quoted in They Had a Dream *by Jules Archer.*

" That day, for a moment, it almost seemed that we stood on a height, and could see our inheritance; perhaps we could make the kingdom real, perhaps the beloved community would not forever remain the dream one dreamed in agony.... "

The black author, James Baldwin, writing about the March on Washington DC, quoted in Let the Trumpet Sound *by Stephen Oates.*

When King surveyed the wreckage of the Sixteenth Street Baptist Church and thought about the loss of innocent young lives he wondered if the struggle was worth it.

the 'Farce on Washington', while other black protestors said the event had been manipulated by the government to portray a racially united country. For a few weeks, the wave of optimism drowned out such claims. Then, on 15 September 1963, the bombing by white extremists of the Sixteenth Street Baptist Church in Birmingham killed four little girls, injured 21 other children and triggered further riots and violence. King was devastated. For the first time he questioned his own beliefs as he realized the difficulty of keeping violence out of the struggle. Was there any hope for his dream?

President Lyndon Johnson shakes King's hand at the signing of the civil rights act on 3 July 1964.

WITHIN A FEW MONTHS OF that memorable afternoon in the White House, President John F. Kennedy was dead. For many people, Kennedy's assassination in Dallas, Texas on 22 November 1963 marked the end of the American dream. In a statement King said that the president's death was 'a great loss to America and the world....' At the same time, he recognized that the sickness of society was to blame for the murder of a president, and he told Coretta his fears that the same would happen to him. He was also concerned about the trustworthiness of President Lyndon Baines Johnson, Kennedy's successor. Johnson moved swiftly to reassure King, and promised to continue Kennedy's work on civil rights. By July 1964, President Johnson had pushed the civil rights act through Congress.

King was invited to the White House to sign the new act that prohibited discrimination in voting, education, employment, housing, and rented accommodation. As King smiled for the camera, he was mindful that the passing of this act wasn't the end of the fight. Johnson believed that the time for demonstration was over, but King's next objective was for economic equality. Even though the signs saying 'whites only' had been withdrawn from lunch counters throughout the country, most black people still couldn't afford to buy a meal in those places. King sensed the rising tide of resentment and proposed a Bill of Rights for the Disadvantaged. He also recognized that, as long as Johnson didn't exercise his authority, the fight for segregation and voter rights would continue.

In October 1964, King was awarded the Nobel Peace Prize. At the age of 35 he was the youngest man ever to receive the award. In his acceptance speech he paid homage to all those who had fought peacefully for civil rights. It was a fitting comment on such an occasion, but the war for civil rights was about to grow bloodier.

In January 1965, King embarked on a campaign for voter registration in Selma, Alabama. On his arrival in Selma he was attacked in the lobby of his hotel. He was arrested and imprisoned as he took part in peaceful marches and he witnessed the terror tactics employed by local police and members of the Klan against black demonstrators. In the face of such brutality, radical black groups demanded more extreme action. Despite criticisms of his methods, and death threats from the Klan, King planned a Selma-to-Montgomery march. In February 1965, Malcolm X was assassinated by Black Muslim extremists. King felt sure it would be his turn next, but he saw the campaign in Selma through to the end. In August, President Johnson passed the voting rights act of 1965. It ruled that federal officials be employed by each district, and anyone attempting to prevent voter registration would be arrested. At last, the promises of democracy had, in some part, been made real.

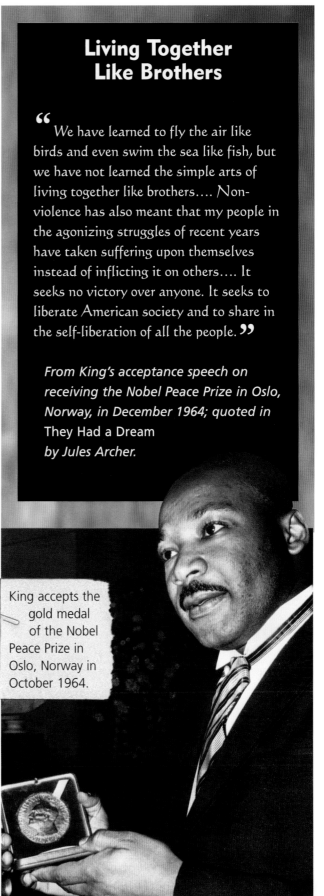

Living Together Like Brothers

" We have learned to fly the air like birds and even swim the sea like fish, but we have not learned the simple arts of living together like brothers.... Non-violence has also meant that my people in the agonizing struggles of recent years have taken suffering upon themselves instead of inflicting it on others.... It seeks no victory over anyone. It seeks to liberate American society and to share in the self-liberation of all the people. "

From King's acceptance speech on receiving the Nobel Peace Prize in Oslo, Norway, in December 1964; quoted in They Had a Dream *by Jules Archer.*

King clasps the hand of his wife on the Selma to Montgomery March in 1965. King was pleased that so many clergymen of different faiths and creeds were there to demonstrate for the black vote.

King accepts the gold medal of the Nobel Peace Prize in Oslo, Norway in October 1964.

Despite the shifts in the civil rights movement, King continued his non-violent protest.

'Power is the only thing respected in this world,' said Stokely Carmichael the spokesman of the Black Power movement, 'and we must get it at any cost.'

FIVE DAYS AFTER THE VOTING rights act was signed, the first major black riot of the 1960s broke out in Los Angeles' Watts ghetto. This time people were fighting against black unemployment and poverty, they were protesting against inferior education and poor housing, and they were demonstrating against the war in Vietnam. Within six days, 34 people had been killed, 850 had been injured, 4,000 had been arrested and 209 buildings had been destroyed. On 17 August, King flew out to Los Angeles to try to calm the riots. It was almost two years since he had stood on a podium at the Lincoln Memorial and pleaded: 'Let us not seek to satisfy our thirst for freedom by drinking from the cup of bitterness and hatred.' Since then, King's own ideas had shifted. He did not condemn the rioters, instead he blamed their actions on poverty and deprivation, and he believed these to be the symptoms of racism.

In the final years of his life, King broadened the horizons of his own dream. He attended demonstrations opposing the Vietnam War and, in 1967, began organizing a 'Poor People's Campaign'. This time he planned a march on Washington DC for disadvantaged people of all races. In some ways he had become more radical; there were also changes within the civil rights movement itself as new, more militant, voices were being heard. Stokely Carmichael left the SNCC to become spokesman for the Black Power movement, and Bobby Seale founded the Black Panthers. Both groups criticized King, accusing him of being out of touch with the needs of the movement. Their aggressive rhetoric and defiant cries of 'Black Power!' seemed to have more relevance for the new generation of black youth who demanded improvements now – by right!

In 1967 there were more riots in cities throughout the US, including New York, Detroit, Michigan and Chicago. In Detroit, tanks and machine-guns were turned on the rioters, and more than 40 people were killed. King dismissed the Black Power movement; as a religious man, he believed in non-violence for the rest of his life. 'If every Negro in the United States turns to violence,' he wrote in response to the Black Power movement, 'I will choose to be that one lone voice preaching that this is the wrong way.'

On 28 March 1968, King arrived in Memphis, Tennessee to lead a march of 6,000 black refuse workers who were striking over discrimination in pay. As the march began, a large crowd of Black Power supporters started smashing shop windows. King called off the march, but in the riot that followed a black teenager was killed and more than 280 people were arrested. King was rushed away under police escort but returned to Memphis again on 3 April. On the plane journey there he talked about threats on his life, and when he took the stage to speak to refuse workers that night he gave the most strangely prophetic speech of his life (see panel on this page). The next evening, at 6.01 pm, as King stood alone on the balcony of the Lorraine Motel, a single rifle shot hit him in the head. At 7.05 pm that night, the father of the civil rights movement was pronounced dead. Two months later, an escaped white convict called James Earl Ray was arrested and charged with the murder of Martin Luther King, Jr.

The Promised Land

" *Well, I don't know what will happen now; we've got some difficult days ahead. But it really doesn't matter with me now, because I've been to the mountaintop. And I don't mind. Like anybody, I would like to live a long life – longevity has its place. But I'm not concerned about that now. I just want to do God's will. And He's allowed me to go up to the mountain. And I've looked over, and I've seen the promised land. I may not get there with you. But I want you to know tonight, that we, as a people, will get to the promised land. And I'm happy tonight. I'm not worried about anything. I'm not fearing any man. Mine eyes have seen the glory of the coming of the Lord.* "

From King's speech to the refuse workers on 3 April 1968, the day before his assassination. Quoted in The Autobiography of Martin Luther King, Jr., *edited by Clayborne Carson.*

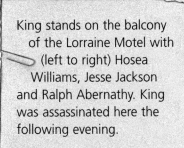

King stands on the balcony of the Lorraine Motel with (left to right) Hosea Williams, Jesse Jackson and Ralph Abernathy. King was assassinated here the following evening.

Dr Martin Luther King, Jr. was laid to rest in Atlanta, Georgia. The words carved on his crypt are from his famous 'I have a dream' speech:

> 'Free at last, free at last,
> Thank God Almighty
> I'm free at last.'

In the last months of his life, in the face of mounting criticism and death threats, King had expressed weariness with the fight. In a speech made on Christmas Eve 1967, he even admitted that not long after giving the 'I have a dream' speech, he saw the dream turn into a nightmare. But in the years since his death, the dream lives on as millions of African Americans have fought as individuals, or as part of the civil rights movement, for equal opportunities and better lives.

Part of the dream has been realized, as black Americans make progress in education and employment. By 1996, 44 per cent of employed blacks held 'white collar' jobs in managerial, professional and administrative positions, rather than jobs in the service sector or manual labour. In the same year, 23 per cent of blacks between the ages of 18 and 24 enrolled at college, compared with 15 per cent in 1983. Blacks have also found a voice in politics – as voters and politicians. Since the federal enforcement of voter registration in 1965, the number of black voters has increased by more than 4 million in the South alone. As a result, more black politicians, officials and mayors have been elected in cities throughout the US.

In 1992 three black candidates – Jesse Jackson, Governor Douglas Wilder and General Colin Powell – ran in the primary elections for the United States presidency. Powell has since been appointed secretary of state by President George W. Bush (elected in 2001), and many Americans agree that he would make a popular president in the future. Black women have also made their mark – Professor Condoleeza Rice, national security advisor to George W. Bush, aspires to the presidency herself.

A simple farm wagon carries the body of Dr. Martin Luther King, Jr. on the funeral procession through Atlanta on 9 April 1968.

A young boy leads a parade in Richmond, Virginia, as part of the Martin Luther King, Jr., Holiday Mass Meeting on 21 January 2002.

More Still To Do

"If Martin Luther King … were to reappear by my side today and give us a report card on the last 25 years, what would he say? You did a good job, he would say, voting and electing people who formerly were not electable because of the color of their skin. You have more political power, and that is good. You did a good job, he would say, letting people who have the ability to live wherever they want to live, go wherever they want to go in this great country. You did a good job, he would say, elevating people of color into the ranks of the United States armed forces to the very top or into the very top of our Government… good job creating a black middle class of people who are doing well…. But, he would say, I did not live and die to see the American family destroyed. I did not live and die to see young people destroy their own lives with drugs… the freedom to die before you're a teenager is not what Martin Luther King lived and died for. "

Former US President Bill Clinton speaking to 5,000 ministers in Memphis, Tennessee on 13 November 1993. The address was made from the pulpit from which Martin Luther King, Jr. gave his last speech.
From The Penguin Book of Twentieth Century Speeches.

In his first speech as South African president Nelson Mandela paid homage to those who had struggled for freedom around the world: 'Their dreams have become reality,' he said. 'Freedom is their reward.'

Much has been achieved since the dark days of the 1960s, but for many black Americans the nightmare continues. The average income of blacks is still lower than that of whites, and black unemployment remains higher too. Many black Americans still live on the breadline in urban neighbourhoods where drugs and crime all too often become the way out for young people who have no prospects. To some, the only method of protest seems to be violent. This fact was demonstrated in the riots of 1992 which broke out in Los Angeles after four policemen who had brutally beaten a young black man called Rodney King were acquitted of the assault. Dr Martin Luther King, Jr. had despaired at the riots that broke out in that city in 1965. Had he been alive, King would have condemned the violence but he would have recognized the conditions that caused it. The riots of the 1990s were a wake-up call to all Americans that the problems caused by racism have not gone away. And, until the day that racism dies, King's dream of racial equality will be a continuing quest until it is achieved.

Glossary

activist Someone who takes action, sometimes military, to bring political change.

appeal To apply to a higher court for the reconsideration of a decision or sentence made in a lower court.

attorney general The chief legal officer in some countries, including the USA.

Baptist A follower of the Christian faith who believes in the necessity of baptism, usually of adults, by dipping them in water.

Black Muslim A member of a political and religious movement that practises Islam and seeks to establish a black nation.

Black Panther A member of a militant black political party that was founded in 1965 to end the political domination of whites.

Black Power A political movement of black people to obtain equality with whites.

boycott To refuse to have dealings with a person or an organization i.e. by refusing to buy products from a shop.

civil rights The rights to equality and justice, particularly those fought for by black people in the USA.

colonists People who settle in another country and impose the rules of their own country on that land.

communism A political system in which private ownership is abolished, and all property is owned by the people.

Confederacy A union of peoples, states etc. In this sense, used to describe the Confederate States of America that withdrew from the Union in 1861.

Congress The US Congress is composed of the Senate and the House of Representatives, and its members propose and vote on new laws.

conspiracy theories Ideas, usually based on guess-work, of how an event really happened.

constitutional rights Rights that belong to a person by the law of the land.

democracy A political system in which the rulers of a state are voted in by the people they rule.

desegregation Ending racial segregation in public places.

discrimination The unfair treatment of a person, ethnic group or minority.

Great Depression A worldwide depression during the 1930s when there was mass unemployment.

federal government The national government of the USA.

federal troops Soldiers enlisted by the government.

ghetto An area of a city where a group of poor people, usually of one race or colour, live together.

integrated Joined together.

interracial Affecting different races of people.

intimidation Frightening or bullying somebody into doing something they don't want to do.

Jim Crow laws The laws of racial segregation that were imposed between the 1880s and the 1960s in many US states. Jim Crow was the name of a black character in a minstrel show.

Ku Klux Klan A secret organization of white US southerners who use violence against blacks, Jews and other minority groups.

legislation The laws of a country.

literacy tests Exams or tests to determine how well a person can read and write.

loitering Acting as though you have nothing to do.

lunch counter Another word for a cafeteria.

lynching The execution by hanging of a person for an offence that has not been tried by jury.

Methodist A member of the Protestant faith who follows the teachings of the English preacher, John Wesley, the founder of Methodism.

migrate The movement of people from one country or region to settle in another.

Negro Another word for black person.

Nobel Peace Prize An award given each year to the person or organization that has made the greatest contribution to world peace.

orator A public speaker.

oratory The art of speaking in public.

pacifism The belief that violence is never acceptable.

pacifist Someone who believes in peace, not war.

parsonage The house in which a parson (priest) lives.

passive resistance Peaceful demonstration, or non-violent resistance, against a government or law.

pastor A priest in charge of a congregation.

pilgrimage The journey to worship at a holy place.

poll tax A tax which is levied on each adult of a country, irrespective of income.

prophetic Predicting the future.

Republican One of the two main US political parties.

rhetoric Written or spoken words that aim to persuade or influence people.

right-wing extremists People with extreme political views, who are especially opposed to rapid change.

sanctioned Something that has been authorized by law.

secretary of state In the USA, the head of the government department in charge of foreign affairs.

segregation The separation of different racial groups.

sermon A religious speech given in church.

sit-in A form of protest in which demonstrators occupy seats in a public place and refuse to move.

theology The study of religion and religious beliefs.

thesis An idea that is debated and proved, usually in written form, as part of a university degree.

Union, the The twenty-three Northern states of the USA that opposed the seceding of the Confederate states during the American Civil War.

US Supreme Court The highest federal court in the USA, which exercises jurisdiction over lower state courts and decides cases to interpret the Constitution.

white supremacy The theory that white people are superior to people of other races.

Further Information

Reading

Free at Last: The Story of Martin Luther King by Angela Bull (Dorling Kindersley, 2000)

Leading Lives: Martin Luther King (Heinemann, 2002)

Lives and Times: Martin Luther King, Jr. by Barraclough, Roop, Woodhouse (Heinemann, 2001)

The March on Washington: Journey to Freedom by L. S. Summer (Child's World Inc., 2000)

Martin Luther King by Christine Hatt (Evans Brothers Limited, 2002)

Tell Me About: Martin Luther King by John Malam (Evans Brothers, 2002)

Sources

The Autobiography of Martin Luther King, Jr. edited by Clayborne Carson (Abacus, 1999)

Black History for Beginners by Denise Dennis (Writers and Readers Publishing Inc, 1995)

I May Not Get There With You: The True Martin Luther King Jr. by Michael Eric Dyson (The Free Press, 2000)

Let the Trumpet Sound: A Life of Martin Luther King by Stephen B. Oates (Payback Press, 1998)

Martin and Malcolm and America by James H. Cone (HarperCollins, 1991)

The Penguin Book of Twentieth Century Speeches edited by Brian MacArthur (Penguin, 1999)

The Sixties by Arthur Marwick (Oxford University Press, 1998)

Slavery: From Renaissance to Today by Milton Meltzer (Cowies Book Company Inc., 1972)

They Had a Dream: The Civil Rights Struggle from Frederick Douglass to Marcus Garvey to Martin Luther King and Malcolm X by Jules Archer (Viking, 1993)

Websites (also used as sources)

http://www.angelfire.com/pa/marchonwashington/march.html

http://www.abbeville.com/civilrights/washington.asp

Timeline

15 January 1929 Martin Luther King Jr., is born in Atlanta, Georgia.

18 June 1953 King marries Coretta Scott.

31 October 1954 King becomes pastor at Dexter Avenue Baptist Church, Montgomery, Alabama.

5 June 1955 King receives his PhD in theology from Boston University.

17 November 1955 Yolanda, King's first child, is born.

5 December 1955 The Montgomery bus boycott begins, King is appointed president of the Montgomery Improvement Association (MIA).

30 January 1956 A bomb is thrown on to the porch of King's house.

21 December 1956 Following the US Supreme Court ruling that segregation of Montgomery's buses is unconstitutional, King, accompanied by Rosa Parks and Ralph Abernathy, takes the first integrated bus ride through Montgomery.

8 January 1957 The Southern Christian Leadership Conference (SCLC) is created. King later becomes its president.

17 May 1957 King leads a march called the 'Prayer Pilgrimage' to Washington DC.

23 October 1957 Martin Luther King III, King's second child, is born.

January 1960 King returns to Atlanta and becomes co-pastor at his father's church, Ebenezer Baptist Church.

February 1960 Students in Greensboro, North Carolina, stage a sit-in at the lunch counter of a Woolworths' store.

April 1960 The Student Non-violent Co-ordinating Committee (SNCC) is formed.

24 June 1960 King meets presidential candidate John F. Kennedy for the first time.

30 January 1961 Birth of Dexter Scott, King's third child.

14 May 1961 First freedom rides set off for New Orleans.

27 July 1962 King is jailed in Albany, Georgia.

28 March 1963 Birth of Bernice, King's fourth child.

12 April 1963 King is jailed in Birmingham, Alabama.

May 1963 Police turn fire hoses and dogs on children on the streets of Birmingham, Alabama.

11 June 1963 President Kennedy announces plans for a civil rights bill.

28 August 1963 King delivers his 'I have a dream' speech at the Lincoln Memorial.

22 November 1963 President John F. Kennedy is assassinated in Dallas, Texas.

3 December 1963 King meets the new president, Lyndon B. Johnson, to discuss the civil rights bill.

2 July 1964 King is present at the signing of the civil rights act by President Johnson.

10 December 1964 King receives the Nobel Peace Prize.

21 February 1965 Malcolm X is assassinated.

21-25 March 1965 King leads the Selma to Montgomery March.

February 1966 King moves to Chicago.

27 November 1967 King launches the 'Poor People's Campaign' and starts to organize a march on Washington.

28 March 1968 King leads a march in Memphis, Tennessee, to support striking refuse collectors.

4 April 1968 King is assassinated at the Lorraine Motel, Memphis.

2 November 1983 King's birthday is designated a public holiday in the USA.